Lifting

MW00941678

How to Support a Loved One with Depression

By K.W. Williams

Copyright 2017 by K W. Williams

Published by Make Profits Easy LLC

Profitsdaily123@aol.com

facebook.com/MakeProfitsEasy

Table of Contents

Introduction

Depression is debilitating. It is a black pit of darkness that individuals can't just shake off or get over. It affects work performance, relationships, sexual performance, and even the sufferer's health. It can literally immobilize a person, stripping away all of the things that he loves, enjoys, and cares about. Sometimes depression can even render someone catatonic or unable to get out of bed. Watching a loved one fall into this dark pit of misery can be just as painful as dealing with depression yourself.

If you live with a person who suffers from depression, the pain is not just theirs. It can be very hard to live with someone who suffers from depression. You may even start to feel depressed yourself as you deal with anger, mood swings, and despondency from your loved one. Seeing your loved one's pain can be extremely painful for you.

It is best to not give up or feel helpless, however. You may think that there is nothing that you can do for someone who suffers from chronic depression, but you actually do more than you realize just by being there. You may keep trying and you feel useless in aiding your loved one through his or her suffering; this book will show you plenty of ways that you can actually become very useful in getting your loved one well. This book will show you how to do the best that you can for your loved one. You can relieve his or her pain and help him or her get better.

This book will also teach you how to cope with the overwhelming stress and pain of having a mentally ill loved one. It certainly is not an easy task to have someone close to you go through depression. You need to care for yourself as well as your loved one. Learn how to relax and provide yourself self-care as you endure your loved one's suffering as well.

Understand that you are not a therapist or a psychiatrist. You cannot cure your loved one of depression. But you can certainly make his life easier. Don't put too much on yourself. Just be there for your loved one, and learn how to adjust your communication and your feelings toward your loved one to become more conducive to his healing. Feelings of anger, resentment, and even blame toward your loved one are perfectly natural. You are not a horrible person for feeling this way. However, you must learn to curb these negative emotions for your loved one as well as your own peace of mind. This book will show you how to work through the anger and sadness that can surround a relationship with a person with depression.

Don't make the mistake of thinking that you are not a valuable tool in your loved one's healing. Being supportive is the best thing that you can do. When the going gets hard, this book is your best friend. Also remember that you are not alone and there are many community resources available to you. Reach out to others for help and always pick up this book when you need some advice or encouragement. So far, you are doing awesome, and you are a great person for trying to continue a relationship with a depression sufferer. Many people would have left already. So my hat is off to you. Just hang in there.

Chapter 1: Understanding Depression

If you want to help your loved one, it is often best if you gain a thorough understanding of what depression is and how it works. This chapter is a crash course in the different types of depression, how they are usually treated, and the symptoms that appear.

What Is Depression?

Depression is a mental illness that affects one's mood, outlook on life, participation in activities, social interaction, and ability to carry out the daily tasks of living. Depression can have very severe effects on a person's life and can lead to self-harm or even suicide. Fortunately, it is also treatable and some people have been able to totally cure their depression altogether.

While there are many causes of depression, most people agree that depression is caused by an imbalance of chemicals within the brain. Dopamine, norepinephrine, and serotonin are neuro-chemicals that are responsible for sleep, happiness, and energy. An imbalance in these chemicals can lead to mood and sleep problems. These imbalances are triggered by anxiety, a trauma, stress, genetics, or even poor lifestyle. Medication and therapy are often effective at correcting this chemical imbalance. Vitamins, minerals, good diet, and exercise also help depression a lot by correcting deficiencies that can contribute to these imbalances.

If you know someone who is depressed, you probably notice that this person won't cheer up, no matter how hard you try. He may stuff his face with junk food but refuse the healthy, nutritious meals that you prepare. He may fail to go to work or school, and may have trouble getting out of bed. He won't want to see friends or do things that he used to love. You might witness him abusing drugs or alcohol, lashing out in violent anger, or simply refusing to participate in life. It can feel like he's pushing you away, but understand that this is a normal symptom of depression and that it really has nothing to do with you personally.

Different Types

There are various types of depression. Not all depression is the same, or else it would be much easier to treat and even cure. Depression affects each individual differently. There are also many different types of depression, with symptoms that differ slightly because of their causes.

Major Depressive Disorder

This is the most common type of depression. People with major depressive disorder have had symptoms for longer than two weeks and are depressed more often than not. They might have good days, but a majority of the time they have bad days. Lack of interest in activities that they enjoy, trouble sleeping, chronic fatigue, general feelings of sadness or anger, and unexplained weight gain or loss are all common signs of major depressive disorder.

Dysthymia

Dysthymia is a mild form of depression that can persist for up to years. While it is not always as devastating as more severe depression, it can greatly lessen a person's quality of life. People with dysthymia are often in a low or negative mood and don't have much energy or joy. They may engage in substance abuse or overeating to try to comfort their symptoms, usually unsuccessfully.

Bipolar Depression

Bipolar depression is the debilitating downswing, or depressive side, of manic depressive disorder, now more commonly referred to as bipolar. Bipolar patients will experience periods of mania, where they have tons of energy and poor impulse control. But what goes up must come down. Eventually, the manic phase ends and bipolar sufferers crash into depression. Often this depression is severe and leads to suicidal thoughts and a total inability to function in life. Sometimes depressive periods are accompanied with psychotic symptoms, like hearing voices or hallucinations. Also, often bipolar individuals engage in self-harm, promiscuity, impulsive behavior, and substance abuse.

Seasonal Affective Disorder (SAD)

The acronym is apt for describing this type of depression, which is brought about during certain seasons or certain types of weather. This depression only appears during cloudy weather, winter, or other seasons that are triggers for the individual. The cool thing about this depression is that it can treated by light therapy, where an individual is exposed to light. It can also be treated by low doses of antidepressants only during the troublesome seasons. When the seasons change, this depression often lifts.

Psychotic Depression

People with psychotic depression exhibit the symptoms of depression but they also suffer from hallucinations, delusions, and paranoia. People with psychotic depression don't see reality clearly, which can lead to their depression as they think that everyone is out to get them. They are at high risk of hurting themselves or others. Their psychotic symptoms should be treated with antipsychotic medications, while their depression should be address with antidepressants.

Postpartum Depression

This is a black hole of depression that women may fall into following a pregnancy. The stress of a new baby as well as the fluctuations in hormones in a woman's body can cause her depression. Postpartum depression can even cause mothers to want to hurt their babies or to reject their babies. Fortunately, this can be treated with vitamins, exercise, and medication. Postpartum depression is possible to cure completely.

Situational Depression

People who can't handle stress or bad emotions well will develop depression in response to bad events in their lives. A bad day, an argument with a loved one, or a break-up can throw situational depression sufferers into a miserable tailspin. Therapy can be helpful in teaching these people to cope with stressful life events better.

Persistent Depressive Disorder

Persistent Depression refers to people who suffer from depression for two years or longer. Their mental state appears to be chronically depressed. Their depression may be light (dysthymia) or it may be crippling chronic major depression. This depression does not just go away on its own, but instead appears to haunt a person constantly.

Premenstrual Dysphoric Disorder (PDD)

This type of depression only affects women. It is caused by an imbalance in hormones related to a woman's menstruation. This is like PMS, but far more severe. Often this type of depression can be treated with hormonal therapies or hormonal birth control. Sometimes it goes away on its own.

Common Causes of Depression

If you have a loved one who suffers from depression, it is not your fault. Even if you feel that his or her moods somehow are personal against you, they are not. Depression is a mental illness that is beyond your control and the sufferer's control. They can't just get over it, and you can't just fix it. I know that that information can be hard to hear, and it can make you feel powerless, but depression is a common mental illness. Millions of Americans are affected every day.

Anxiety Leads to Depression

Many people who suffer from depression also suffer from another mental disorder. This is known as co-morbidity. The most common disorder that accompanies depression is anxiety. Anxiety causes a person to see the worst in everything and always live in a state of exaggerated fear and worry for no good reason. Of course this is very negative, and it can lead to depression, as the person loses hope and expends too much energy on being miserable and nervous.

There are many different types of anxiety. Most people with anxiety suffer from generalized anxiety disorder. This is where someone experiences anxiety often about most life situations. Other people may suffer from social anxiety, where they fear social interaction and become obsessed with how they look to others. Finally, there is panic disorder, which can cause panic attacks. Panic attacks are traumatizing and can often contribute to depression.

Lifestyle

How your loved one lives can be a major factor in his mental health. A poor lifestyle is a common source of depression. If he does not eat right or take care of his body right, this can cause an imbalance in the chemicals in his brain. Correcting his lifestyle may at least help his depression. Sometimes it may entirely undo his depression.

Genes

Sometimes, the propensity for depression lies in the genetics of a person. Depression and also anxiety can be passed down from family member to family member. A look into the health history of someone's family will reveal if they have inherited depression. Almost all people with depression have indeed inherited the tendency for it. This is why some people will endure trauma, stress, or poor lifestyle without ever getting depression, while others who strive to be positive and healthy still cannot shake off depression symptoms.

Medication and therapy are usually best for helping someone get over a natural predisposition for depression. Coping skills taught in therapy can help him learn to handle the symptoms when they arise, without wanting to die. You can also be a positive influence on him to help him feel better. Teach him how to gather a positive support network that will carry him through the painful moments when his mental illness gets the best of him. It is also incredibly important that he leads a healthy lifestyle and gets into habits that are conducive to better mental health.

Trauma

Depression often arises after someone experiences something horrible. Seeing the worst that can possibly happen will undoubtedly affect someone's mental outlook on life. A trauma can rob someone of his ability to think positively and to look at life with hope.

There are many different types of trauma. Rape, attempted murder, assault, a near-death experience, the sudden loss of a loved one, miscarriage or stillbirth, and even an emotionally harmful relationship or break-up or divorce are all forms of trauma that can derail your loved one's life and mental health.

Recovering from a trauma is especially difficult since your loved one will probably prefer to repress his emotions and thoughts regarding the trauma. This trauma will cause emotional scars that will continue to manifest in the form of anxiety, depression, suicidal thoughts, social problems, nightmares, and flashbacks.

Addressing the trauma is essential for healing. Repression is never helpful.

Usually, the best treatment for trauma-related depression is intense therapy or psychiatric intervention. Qualified professionals can help your loved one sort through his emotions and thoughts related to the trauma and learn to cope with the after effects. In addition, medication can help him feel better as he learns how to heal. As his loved one, you can play a role by being there and not abandoning him in his time of need.

Chronic Illness

Being sick for a long period of time is not fun for anyone. The effects of illness and being bedridden can naturally disrupt someone's neuro-chemical balance and lead to feelings of dejection, misery, loss, and eventually depression.

Illness or a serious injury can impair someone's ability to live life normally, which can make him feel useless or even like he is better off dead. This can cause him to sink into deep depression as he must face new physical limitations and inabilities. As he sees his former life end because of the new limitations, he may sink into depression.

The best thing to do for someone who has been through a chronic illness is to make him see that life is not over. Offer him reasons to be cheerful, like art, pets, and funny movies. Also, be there to provide him comfort. Even just sitting at the side of his bed holding his hand can provide him a huge source of comfort and relief. Try to find activities that he can still perform even with his new physical limitations.

As someone recovers from a long bout of illness or a serious injury, the process of rehabilitation can be stressful and overwhelming. People who have endured great amounts of suffering may have trouble assimilating into the world again. Physical therapy or other forms of rehabilitation can be very painful and can constantly remind him of how an illness or injury has negatively impacted his life. Again, being there for him throughout this process and reminding him that he can heal is very important for his recovery.

Sad Life Circumstances

Repeated sad life circumstances or stress can destroy someone's confidence, happiness, and peace of mind. Constantly experiencing bad emotions from harsh life circumstances can really tear down one's mood, making him depressed. Mistakes and failures can also erode his self-esteem, making him hate himself and leading to his depressed mood.

It is best to always encourage him to look on the bright side. Help him make better decisions by talking life choices through with him. Let him know that you still love him and think that he is a great person, even despite his regrettable decisions or circumstances in the past. Help him see life events as a learning experience that he can grow from. Distract him from his pain by introducing joy into his life, through fun activities, pets, and the love of family and friends. Also, urge him to exercise and perform other activities to relieve his stress and get his mind off of his misery. Being there for him through his dark times will help him recover and feel better when life finally eases up and things get better.

Dwelling on the Past

Your loved one has no control over the past. Thinking about it too much can really ruin his mood as he can't do anything about events that have passed. Being stuck in the past can really destroy his mood and it is an unhealthy habit that he needs to learn to get over.

Explain to him that the past is over and that he can't change it. Tell him that you believe thinking about the past too much is why he is so depressed. Distract him from his thoughts by taking him out or giving him a task that he can enjoy. Try to discourage him when he starts bringing up the past by telling him, "That's over. Let's think about better things." Also, therapy can really help him get over and work through issues from the past.

Catastrophizing

Catastrophizing is when your loved one blows things out of proportion in his mind. He makes life out to be worse than it really is. This negative thinking can be a source of his depression. But it can also be remedied by more positive thinking habits.

When you catch your loved one blowing things out of proportion, propose that he thinks about things in a calmer way. Ask him, "Is this really the end of the world? Should you invest so much emotional energy into this issue? Is it really that big of a deal?"

Ruminating

Ruminating is the harmful mental habit of thinking too much about one's problems. If your loved one gets caught in a mental loop of thinking about how horrible his life is, he is bringing about his depression. Meanwhile, his depression causes him to ruminate. It's a vicious cycle that must be ended.

Therapy, particularly cognitive behavioral therapy, can teach him to have more helpful, solution-oriented thoughts. It can teach him to reach out to others for comfort and to be more grateful for the good things in life. You can also be a positive influence on him by encouraging him to notice how great life really is.

Other Mental Health Issues

Co-morbidity is the term used to describe when a person has more than one mental disorder affecting him. Your loved one needs to be tested to find out if he has other issues that lead to his depression. Bipolar, anxiety, personality disorders, and schizophrenia can all lead to symptoms that increase his rate of depression. Sometimes, depression is only a symptom of another more serious disorder that disrupts his life and his mood.

Substance Abuse or Other Addictions

Substance abuse is typically a symptom of depression. But the effects of certain substances can really affect someone poorly. They can exacerbate depression severely. Any kind of substance abuse is harmful. Any unhealthy vice that your loved one engages in is likely to add to his depression.

Encourage your loved one to seek help. You may need to stage an intervention of some sort. Convince your loved one about how much he is hurting himself as well as the people who care about him. Also, urge him to seek therapy that helps him uncover the issues that he is trying to bury or numb with substances or other habits.

Abuse

If your loved one was the victim of abuse, then it is likely that he will experience depression later on in life. Abuse is a form of trauma that can leave a permanent stamp on someone's identity and mental health. Victims of abuse have trouble feeling good, forming healthy relationships, and otherwise living their lives normally.

Abuse must be treated with medication and therapy. Therapy is one of the only ways that your loved one can work through his issues and learn to love himself and recognize his own worth. Since his abuser has stripped that away from him, he needs help getting it back. You should also express lots of love and never take his depression or actions of resistance personally. He has been through more than you could ever understand, so be patient with him.

Sex Hormone Issues

Sex hormones can really throw everything off when they are imbalanced. They can really influence the mood and mental health of your loved one.

Pregnancy can lead to worsened or exacerbated mental health issues. Many pregnant women develop OCD, depression, and/or anxiety during their pregnancy. Pregnancy causes sex hormones to go crazy, which can make a pregnant loved one feel very depressed. Stressful circumstances surrounding the pregnancy, such as financial worries, becoming a single mom, or complications with the pregnancy, can add to the depression. Try to offer your pregnant loved one plenty of things to look forward to. Add to her joy about the coming baby by helping her decorate the nursery or pick out cute outfits for the baby. Keep her focused on the bright side.

Certain forms of birth control can also disrupt women's hormones. If you know a female loved one who was never depressed but now is very depressed after starting a new birth control, suggest that she switch birth controls. A visit to the gynecologist may be necessary.

Sometimes, other issues, such as ovarian cysts, can contribute to depression. Reproductive issues must always be ruled out when depression is an issue. Men are not exempt from this, either.

Male hormonal problems related to testicular or prostate issues should be addressed by a doctor.

Menopause, menstruation, and PMS are also times when women may experience more depression. Usually, this form of depression will ease when the hormonal issues are over. However, you still need to provide support for a woman who is experiencing depression because of a hormonal issue. Bring her dark chocolate and take her out for a good time.

The Seasons and Weather

SAD is a very common form of depression that is influenced by the climate. Your loved one may only suffer during certain times. Most people who have SAD get sick with depression during winter months, or months when there is little light.

Light therapy can help people who grow depressed because of persistent darkness. This therapy exposes SAD sufferers to light, helping regulate the chemicals in their brains. Medication can also be useful. Try to get your loved one out and give him things to look forward to in the months or days when his depression is triggered by weather. Just walking outside during winter can help him feel better, for example. Make sure that he does not stay trapped in his home during the weather periods that make him sick.

Nutrient Deficiencies

Depression can be caused by a mere deficiency in some vital nutrient. Nutritional deficiencies can be spotted using blood panels. They can be corrected with proper diet and supplements. I go over diet and supplements in Chapter 6. A depressed person can really benefit from adjusting his diet and getting enough proper nutrition.

Dehydration

Sometimes, feelings of low mood and lack of energy are caused simply by a lack of proper hydration. Your loved one needs to be consuming at least eight glasses of water a day. He should also try drinks like Gatorade to gain proper electrolytes and hydration. Sodas, coffee, tea, and alcohol may be liquids, but they have dehydrating properties which make them unsuitable for treating dehydration. It is very important to make sure that your loved one drinks enough water.

Antidepressants and other psychiatric meds can contribute to dry mouth and dehydration. They can fail to work properly if your loved one is severely dehydrated. Make sure that he drinks enough while on these medications.

How to Diagnose Your Loved One

If you are not a certified mental health professional, you cannot diagnose your loved one's mental illness. But as someone who knows this person well, you can spot signs of depression. If you suspect that your loved one has depression, the best thing to do is to make him see a primary care doctor. Primary care doctors are more than capable of diagnosing depression and referring your loved one to a good therapist and psychiatrist. The doctor can also test your loved one's blood to make sure that there are no physical conditions, such as nutrient deficiencies, diabetes, pregnancy, hormonal imbalances, or thyroid issues, which may be underlying his problem. Treating any physical issues can effectively cure his depression or at least begin the road to recovery.

If your loved one already has a diagnosis of depression, then you need to make sure that he seeks proper treatment. He needs a mental health team that can prescribe medications, help him learn coping skills, guide him in working through emotional scars from traumas or stress, and monitor his progress. Sometimes, your loved

one may be in denial and may resist treatment.

Or he may simply not want to go to

appointments or take his meds because

depression prevents him from having the energy

necessary to get well. You can certainly help him

in this regard by accompanying him to

appointments and overseeing his medication

regimen.

Chapter 2: What It's Like Being with Someone with Depression

You probably already know exactly how it feels to be with someone who suffers from depression. However, I will go over many of the signs and common complaints that people in your situation have here. Maybe you will find out that some of your loved one's most hurtful or frustrating behavior is actually quite normal for people with depression. It can be relieving and helpful to thoroughly understand what depression looks like. You can feel less alone, knowing that other people experience the same things that you do.

Just remember that none of this behavior is personally aimed at you. Depression really is an illness. The sufferer does not always do or say nice things, but he doesn't intend to hurt you. He is simply not himself. The chemical imbalance in his brain that makes him feel so bad also causes him to act out, sometimes in ways that may appear malicious. He may also seem incredibly selfish and unfeeling toward others, but it is hard for people with depression to exit their own heads, so they act selfishly without realizing what they are doing. Depression has been known to make empathy hard in sufferers, so don't take his behavior personally.

Anger

A lot of people erroneously assume that depression is all sadness. But there is a lot of anger involved in depression, too. Depressed individuals may have violent tempers, angry outbursts, or a constantly irritable attitude. This anger can hurt you and make you feel like you can't do anything right. Your home life can become miserable, as you want to avoid this person who is always lashing out at you. The way that his moods rapidly switch can make you feel like you are walking on eggshells around him.

Dealing with this anger can be very emotionally difficult for you. Patience is the best thing to use during this time. Try to de-escalate his angry episodes or avoid him when he is in an angry mood. Be a good listener and encourage him to tell you what he is going through and why he is so mad. He will probably calm down if you show that you care. However, if he doesn't, it is perfectly acceptable for you to protect yourself by

walking away. Again, you are not this persons'
therapist.

If someone becomes violent, it may be
necessary to commit him to a mental health
facility. People who pose risks to themselves or
others are legally supposed to be committed for
psychiatric evaluation and treatment. An
inpatient program can actually do him wonders.
Don't believe the horror stories about mental
hospitals. Many of them are actually relaxing,
healing facilities where electric shock therapy is
not used. Patients are usually held for a few days
for observation while they attend group and
individual therapy, art therapy, yoga, and a
medication regimen. Often, they feel much better
when they leave. They also get to continue seeing
a therapist and psychiatrist through an

outpatient program, to make sure that their medication and therapy continues to work properly. Don't feel bad about committing a very sick loved one if he poses a danger to himself or others.

The same goes for suicide threats. Never neglect to take a suicide threat seriously. All threats must be reported to the police or the patient's psychiatrist. Another great thing about mental hospitals is that they have suicide watches and can prevent a patient from hurting himself.

Despondency

You suggest, "Let's go out dancing tonight!" He frowns and grumbles about not feeling up to it. You are excited for a party, but he just wants to stay in and sleep or watch TV. You may feel like your loved one does not ever want to do anything fun with you. His despondency may certainly bother you and leave you feeling rejected.

But keep in mind that depression robs your loved one of the ability to feel excitement or joy for activities that he once loved. He isn't doing this deliberately. There is no reason why he doesn't want to go out with you, beyond the fact that he doesn't feel up to it because of his depression.

You may also feel rejected as you start to see less of a loved one. He may stop visiting or calling. His Facebook presence may wane, or he may appear active on social media yet he never reaches out and engages with you socially. This is also normal for depressed people. Sometimes you just need to show up at his house, rather than waiting on him to see you. It does not mean that he does not care about you or that you don't matter. He literally is unable to reach out to other people socially, even close loved ones.

Lack of Sex

If your sexual partner is depressed, you might notice a huge drop in his or her sexual performance. Before you start to think that you must be unattractive to this person now, keep in mind that depression causes people to lose interest in things that they love, even sex. Antidepressants also have the side effect of impotency. So you may feel let down by your partner's reticence to get it on, but it really has nothing to do with you. You are not hideous or somehow unattractive to your partner. In fact, the sexual problems that you two have probably embarrasses and bothers your loved one even more than it bothers you.

Strange Behavior

Some of your loved one's behavior might be incredibly strange. You might wonder what is going on in his head as he performs actions that make no sense. He may lack common sense, reason, and logic because depression makes his cognition foggy and poor. You may get frustrated or even scared by your loved one's spaciness and lack of sense, but understand that he is not stupid. He is also not acting out deliberately just to get attention and he is not acting helpless just because he is lazy. His depression really is impairing his judgment and his cognitive abilities.

However, this does not mean that you have to humor and indulge your loved one's every problem. Sometimes, you do need to show some tough love to encourage your loved one to finally get out of his shell and take care of himself. You cannot let him get used to having others think for him and do things for him, especially if he is an adult. However, be gentle. Gently and kindly encourage him to exercise better judgment and to think things through before he acts. Don't just shout at him that he needs to learn to stand on his own two feet. This will backfire as he resists your efforts and becomes more depressed, thinking that everyone hates him.

It's also important to pick your battles. What behavior is tolerable and possible to ignore? What behavior really needs to change for the sanctity of your family? If your loved one engages in some odd behavior or poor judgment that doesn't really hurt anyone, you don't need to micromanage and make him feel like a failure as a human being. Instead, only correct behavior that really does need to change because it poses harm to others, including yourself. Avoid unnecessary criticism and fighting with someone who is depressed. Too much fighting and criticism can simply make his depression worse. Remember that depression impairs one's cognitive and emotional health, so if you offer even light criticism with the best intentions, he may take it very personally and assume that you hate him or he will make some other extreme conclusion. It is best to simply let some things slide. Understand that weird behavior and acting out is all part of depression.

Depression in adolescents can especially result in some odd behavior that you might not be able to understand. Depressed teens are also still growing and finding themselves. Depression hinders them from expressing themselves and enjoying life, so they may enter very dark periods of misery. They may also act out in frustration because they feel so estranged and alienated from other teens who are not depressed. They don't understand themselves or how to manage their depression symptoms so they become very temperamental. As they experiment with how to express themselves and how to cope with their depression, they may go through odd phases or get into strange habits and cliques. These phases are usually normal and you don't need to stress about them too much. Just keep an eye on your teen's behavior and try not to interfere. Let them find themselves and figure out their depression. Offer light guidance, but don't smother your teens, as this will make them resist you and pull away.

Depression can also take on some characteristics of dementia in elderly people, or it may mask the beginning stages of dementia. "Kooky" and bizarre behavior, delusions, and memory problems are all related to depression, but in elderly patients, especially those who have never suffered from depression before, they can be a sign of something more ominous. Be sure to get them checked out by a doctor. And be sure to treat their depression and keep them company a lot. Suicide rates are quite high among elderly patients.

Strange behavior can also be a sign of psychotic depression. If an individual displays psychotic symptoms, like seeing or hearing things that are not there, then you should immediately take him to see a psychiatrist for testing. Find out if he has bipolar, psychotic depression, or some other treatable psychotic disorder like schizophrenia or dissociative identity disorder.

Disordered Sleep

Your loved one may want to sleep all day. Then, at night, he is like a rabid dog, running around the house with lots of energy. You may think that he's being lazy or deliberately trying to keep you up, but in truth depression has flipped his sleep cycle and disrupted his Circadian rhythm. He cannot help being a night owl.

It is a good idea to try to help your loved one's Circadian rhythm if you live with this person. Lights out, TVs off, and computers shut at nine or ten, a half hour before your desired bedtime. Make everyone chamomile tea. Introduce your loved one to melatonin or valerian or some other natural sleep supplement, which cannot be overdosed on and which will not form habits. Also, avoid eating anything at least a half hour before bed, and discourage caffeine use at least six hours before bed.

Substance Abuse

Depression causes sufferers a lot of emotional pain. It is not unusual for depressed people to try to self-medicate with substances. Alcoholism is a common reaction to depression, but unfortunately alcohol can exacerbate depression since it is a depressant. Many depressed people also like stimulants like meth or cocaine, because they falsely believe that stimulants will give them the joy and energy that they lack. Finally, some depressed people want to obliterate their pain completely by using drugs like heroin, pain pills, benzodiazepines, and barbiturates, which help them feel numb and also help them fall asleep. If your loved one start abusing substances, including legal prescription medications, it can be very hard on you as you watch them ruin their lives and their health.

It is not always possible to get a loved one to stop using drugs. But suggest that your loved one attends an inpatient or outpatient rehab program. Also try to introduce your loved one to better friends and healthier pastimes, like yoga or volunteering. Often, depressed people will prefer to engage in healthier activities and get clean and sober when they feel better, so helping your loved one seek depression treatment is also essential to helping them establish sobriety.

If you don't know if your loved one is abusing drugs or not, there are a few ways to tell. Sudden, drastic changes in behavior are often an indication that your loved one is under the influence of something. The inexplicable smell of cat pee, not eating, avoiding social activities, and staying up for days on end is a good indication of meth use. Nasal issues and sore throat can indicate coke use. Frequent stomach problems, nausea, and vomiting for no reason can be caused by opiates. Staring into space, sleeping too much, and having sudden cravings for tons of food can clue you in that your loved one is abusing benzodiazepines, like Xanax or Ativan. Sleeping too much, disappearing for long periods of time with no explanation, run-ins with the law, missing school or work, hostility and irritability, and long periods of inactivity can also indicate the use of drugs.

Unfortunately, these signs are also consistent with the symptoms of depression, so they do not always indicate substance abuse is afoot. Look for more conclusive evidence to back your suspicions. Watch the kinds of people that your loved one hangs out with; like attracts like and drug addicts usually run together. Needle marks or bruises over the veins of the arms can indicate that your loved one is engaging in IV drug use. Finding bottles stashed around the house, needles, and little plastic baggies are good signs that your loved one is self-medicating. You can also nab some hair from his brush for a drug test to get conclusive results.

Odd Eating Habits

You prepare a nice lasagna or luscious salad and he groans and says he's not hungry. Later, you catch him stuffing his face with KFC chicken or ice cream. His preference for junk food over healthy food is not a personal statement about your cooking. Rather, his body is not in proper harmony, so it craves fats and sugars for emotional comfort. He literally craves junk food because of his depression.

On the flipside, your loved one may not want to eat at all. Depression causes some people to under-eat. As the weight falls off of his bones, you may become worried about his health. And you should be. If he doesn't like to eat, you should try to get him psychiatric help immediately before he causes permanent damage to his body.

Sudden Loss of Friends

Your loved one was once a happy-go-luck social person. Suddenly he is breaking with all of his friends. He no longer goes out and he seems to have a lot of falling-outs with people that he once liked. He may complain that he hates everyone, or that everyone hates him. The parties and other social activities that he used to go to are suddenly no longer on his to-do list. Nothing social is on his to-do list, really. He may even start pushing you away, avoiding you, picking fights with you, and accusing you of not being a good person or of hating him. You never did anything to him, yet suddenly he seems to hate you.

Your loved one is probably going through a tough time because of his depression. Refusing to leave is the best thing that you can do for him. Tell him that you understand what he is going through and that you are not leaving his side because you really do love him and find him worthy of your attention. Tell him that you're not like everyone else; you're not going to just leave.

He will appreciate this more than you know, even if he grumbles or acts like he doesn't care about your friendship.

Suicidal Ideation or Attempts

You don't want to wait until your loved one actually attempts suicide to get help. If he is exhibiting suicidal ideation, you need to listen. A lot of people make the mistake of thinking that frequent talk about suicide and suicide threats are just cries for attention. Indeed, they are, but your loved one needs this attention. He needs help and he needs to feel loved. Don't take these threats lightly and don't ignore them thinking that they mean nothing. Maybe your loved one has never acted on one of his suicide threats before, but the very fact that suicide is on his mind is disturbing and indicates that there is a serious problem.

You may also feel that your loved one is just trying to hurt you with these threats. Of course these threats are painful to you, but your loved one probably does not mean to hurt you. Even if he does, threatening suicide in order to hurt someone is not normal. He needs serious psychiatric help if he is doing this to you, and you need to free yourself from this pain.

Not only do you need to protect your loved one, but you also need to protect yourself. You can be held legally liable if your loved one makes a threat that you ignore and then actually does harm himself. You can be charged with criminal negligence if you don't act on his suicide threats.

The best thing to do is to call the police the minute your loved one makes a threat. The police will commit him to a mental hospital for at least three days, depending on the laws in your state. While this may seem harsh, your loved one needs help and he also needs to learn that making suicide threats is not OK.

If your loved one has suicidal thoughts but doesn't make threats, encourage your loved one to talk to a counselor and to also talk to you. Let him know that you don't judge and that you are there for him. If he is feeling suicidal, you want to help him stay alive and safe.

Self-harm

Burning, cutting, self-mutilation, self-strangulation, and other forms of self-harm are alarming signs that your loved one is suffering a lot emotionally. He is using self-harm to relieve his pain through the natural endorphins that injuries release. These endorphins create a brief but powerful high that helps him get away from his emotional pain for a while. He is also trying to let you know that he doesn't care about his health or safety and that he might actually do something worse than just injuring his skin next time.

Self-harm calls for some serious intervention. It's best to get your loved one into counseling if you can. Report what you have seen so that his counselor can help him, since he might not want to share details about his self-harm himself. Also, keep a close eye on him to make sure that he does not continue to engage in the behavior. Sometimes, a mental hospital visit may also be in order.

Poor Hygiene

If it is hard to get out of bed, then it may be even harder for individuals with depression to get into the shower. A lack of hygiene and a messy room or house are two very disgusting and annoying behaviors that your loved one might start showing. It may seem that he no longer cares, and in a way that is true. He cares in his heart, but he simply doesn't have the energy or the willpower to keep up his appearance and his home. Doing the dishes, making the bed, and showering are all activities that can be overwhelming for people with depression. Don't call your loved one lazy or gross. Instead, offer to help them clean up a little sometimes.

You may also notice that a female family member who used to care about her appearance suddenly stops applying makeup, doing her hair, and coordinating outfits. Suddenly, she slacks in her appearance and wanders around in pajamas. Take her out for a spa day or a makeover and see how that helps her cheer up. Don't just criticize her for looking bad, for she probably already knows but doesn't have the energy to change.

It can be very helpful to take elderly loved ones to the barber shop or salon. The difference this makes can be amazing. As elderly people enjoy themselves and regain their pride with improvements to their appearances, they also start to feel better. The same thing can work for a slovenly and depressed teen.

Physical Changes

Depression is a real disease. It not only pilfers the mind of healthy chemicals like serotonin and dopamine, but it also harms the physical body. The chemical imbalance that causes depression also causes various health issues. The stress hormones cortisol and adrenalin may also be present in individuals who are depressed because they are also anxious or else they are suffering from the situational variety of depression.

You will notice weight gain or weight loss. You will notice that your loved one often complains of headaches and muscle aches. You will notice bags under your loved one's eyes as his sleep cycle is continually disrupted. Finally, you will notice that your loved one is listless with no energy. His body seems to lag as he walks. He doesn't have the same pep in his step. You will notice gaps in hygiene and careless dressing. An overall appearance of drooping is common. Tension in the shoulders is also common.

Chapter 3: What You Can Do as a Loved One

Maybe you do feel helpless as you watch, and pretty much join, your loved one fight the battle against mental illness. It certainly may seem like you have no control and you are not doing much to help. As you attempt to get your loved one to change his behavior and fail to have an effect on how he acts, you may feel that your efforts are all in vain.

But in fact, just the fact that you are there and that you have not yet left is admirable. You are actually doing a lot. Continue to be there for your loved one, and you are a hero. Not all heroes wear capes. I am proud of you for standing strong and helping someone through so much at the expense of your own happiness.

Now here are some tips that can help you become a better pillar of support for someone depressed. Some of your actions may be well-intended, but they will backfire on you. Learning how to properly act toward your loved one for the ultimate best results is a good idea.

Avoid Tough Love

Tough love is often a misguided attempt to goad depressed people into better behavior by using threats, coldness, reverse psychology, and ultimatums like "If you keep staying in bed, I'm leaving." The intention is to get someone to change their behavior. But the result is often the opposite. You can be unintentionally hurtful and you can deepen your loved one's depression exponentially with this approach.

Instead of tough love, use gentle words of love. When your loved one does something that infuriates you, remind yourself that this is just part of his or her illness and try to ignore it. Offer to help your loved one; if he refuses, back off. You can't make someone get help unless he threatens or attempts suicide or homicide, in which case you can call the police and have him committed in an inpatient psychiatric ward.

Remember that depression is painful for your loved one. You never want to do anything to increase that pain. Rather, you want to be a source of love and light.

Avoid Criticism and Judgment

Depressed people are often their own harshest critics. You would be amazed at the cruel things that run through the minds of depression sufferers when they think about themselves. Adding to this pain of criticism is usually only throwing salt in the wound. What you criticize or judge is probably already something that a depressed person realized about himself and hates about himself. He can't help it or change it in his emotionally frozen depressed state, however, so he feels helpless. Your criticism only hurts more.

Even if you think you are being constructive with your criticism, you probably are not. It is far better to be nonjudgmental and hold your tongue when it comes to criticism. Stop making suggestions. Stop pointing out what he does wrong. He is already aware of it. Instead, ask him to tell you what is bothering him and help him reach conclusions on his own. Also, urge him to get into therapy. Therapy can help him work out his self-loathing and teach him to love himself more.

If you have frequently been judgmental in the past, this may be why your attempts to help your loved one have failed. It is time to abandon that habit. Your loved one may expect criticism from you, so he may at first resist your attempts to help in other ways. But eventually, he will recognize that you really are trying to help and he will relax. Criticism leads to defensiveness and resentment, so keep this in mind as you try to help. You will have an easier time if you don't try to judge and criticize.

Avoid Minimizing or Dismissing Their Pain

One thing that depressed people truly hate is when others dismiss or somehow downplay their pain. It is easy to want to dismiss a depressed person's pain when you can't feel it yourself. It is easy to say things like, "Oh, just cheer up" or "Just lighten up" or "It's not that bad." But you don't understand how alone and isolated you make your depressed loved one feel when you say things like this. He already feels like no one understands him or identifies with his pain. You just confirmed it. I know that you mean well, but this dismissing and belittling sadly does not work at all.

It is far more helpful if you tell him something like, "I'm sorry you feel this way. I can't identify, but I want to help. I know that you can't just cheer up, but what do you think will make you feel better?" Try to lead him to think of solutions to his misery. Having a solution-oriented mindset can really help him start to cope with depression.

Avoid Giving Advice

Sadly, you are not in your loved one's shoes. Your advice is certainly well-intentioned, but it is also probably not very helpful. If anything, it is probably just frustrating to your loved one. It is best to withhold advice. You cannot correct your loved one's issues just by spouting common sense. Yes, it is common sense for your loved one to get out and to eat better. You can say this all day long, wondering why your loved one refuses to listen. The reason why is because depression undermines common sense.

Also, your loved one probably is not talking to you just to get your advice. Understand the fact that sometimes your loved one just wants to talk to you to vent. If you keep interrupting to offer insight and advice, it can feel very frustrating or even callous to your loved one. Take some time to just listen and let him vent. Don't keep adding your two cents and don't ever interrupt. Just make sympathetic sounds or nod your head to show that you are listening. Stop thinking about what you will say next, and instead let him fill the silence. He will talk more and more and unload a lot if you don't keep interrupting. He will also feel more at ease. Sometimes, you can provide a form of great therapy to your loved ones without even trying. Everyone needs someone to listen to them at least sometimes, especially people with mental health issues who are going through a lot.

Perform Small Acts of Kindness

The small things often mean the most. Doing little gestures to show your loved one that you care can help brighten his day and ease him out of his sense that he is unloved, unlovable, and alone. These beliefs may be irrational and you may think that you show that you care plenty, but understand how negative depression makes people feel. So strive to show that you care even more.

Bring him his favorite soda or flavor of ice cream. Take him to the movies, or the spa. Go swimming together. Or if he is feeling too down to get out, put on his favorite movie and quietly sit there and watch it with him.

Just being there is more essential than you realize. You don't have to do some super exciting activity together or talk about deep things. Sometimes, just sitting there in silence is enough to break up the solitude that rules his life at the moment. He will appreciate it so much, possibly without ever telling or showing you. You will also feel better, knowing that you helped him feel at least a little better.

Accompany Them to Therapy

There is a huge stigma surrounding meds and therapy. Some people can feel quiet embarrassed going to therapy, or they may feel scared of dredging up issues that they don't want to talk about. Many people may even resist therapy, thinking that it marks them as crazy.

You can greatly increase someone's chances of seeking help if you offer to accompany him. You won't be in the actual session, but just going with him to the office and helping him find a good therapist that matches his needs can make him feel more at ease. He will also feel more pressure from you to actually go to an appointment and to stick with therapy.

Lower Your Expectations

While this advice may sound rather harsh, you really do need to lower your expectations. Actually, a better phrase would be "Adjust your expectations." Your loved one really is sick.

Depression is a true illness. Therefore, he has certain limitations on what he can do, just as someone with a broken arm in a cast can't play baseball for at least a few weeks. He won't be able to do everything that a healthy person can because he does not feel well. Always remember that he has limitations, even if he looks normal and well on the outside. You must adjust your expectations as a result and stop expecting or pushing him to do things that are beyond his capability.

It might seem like expecting someone to get out of bed and go through the daily tasks of living is not too much to ask, but for a depressed person, it really is. He can only do so much in his state. Taking baby steps are best. If you want your loved one to be more social, take him to the mall where he can be social without overexerting himself. If you want him to take up exercising, start introducing light exercise to his routine to build him up to the challenge. Don't expect him to be able to suddenly get out and be social, go to work, take care of himself properly, and behave normally overnight just because you ask him to.

If you expect too much of your loved one, you can make him feel like a failure. He may feel like he keeps letting you down. This will only compound the feelings of failure, inadequacy, and unhappiness that he already feels because of his depression.

Have a Life Away from Your Loved One

Your loved one may become hostile or distant as a result of his depression. This can make your relationship with him unfulfilling and tense. Getting away sometimes is essential to preserve your relationship. You need to build a social life aside from your loved one. If your loved one is a romantic partner or spouse, you need to make sure that you spend time with friends and family other than him. If your loved one is your child, try to spend time with other people while he or she is in school. Otherwise, it should be fairly easy to step away from this person for a while.

You accomplish two things by having a social life away from your loved one. The first thing that you accomplish is you give yourself positive social stimulation with healthy people.

This can help you get over the sense that you are somehow repulsive or not good enough for your depressed loved one. These feelings can certainly arise if your loved one is unable to express love to you.

The second thing is that you provide a sort of model for your depressed loved one to follow. You show him that it is possible to go out and have fun and make friends. You show him the importance of making his social life a priority. Through example, teach him how he needs to get out and spend time with people other than you.

If he is too dependent on you because you are his only remaining friend, he probably will experience jealousy when you go out with other people. Simply reassure him that you love him but there are other important people in your life, too. This gently reminds him that he is not the only person in your life and that you are not solely responsible for all of his happiness. It will nudge him toward finding other people to hang out with, leading him to branching out and developing a social network. This social network is one of the key things that will help him recover from a vicious or even chronic bout of depression.

Furthermore, this protects you emotionally and helps you conserve your energy and sanity. You need to experience things other than the depressed energy that your loved one emits. Getting out and having a life away from your depressed loved one helps you expose yourself to better energy for a while. This revitalizes you, so that you come back to your loved one refreshed and in a brighter mood. You can provide better support and care for him if you feel well yourself. Your positivity will be contagious and will help lighten his own dark mood, at least somewhat.

Make it a Team Effort

In many instances throughout this book, I mention harmlessly tricking your loved one into doing things, or leaving hints to motivate him to engage in helpful behaviors. But I only suggest doing this if your loved one absolutely refuses to take action to get well. Before you go about slyly pushing or influencing your loved one, try to forge a team effort with him.

Let him know that you are as interested in seeing him get well as he is. Tell him that you want to work with him and help him achieve mental balance and health. Then, outline a plan that he can agree to. The two of you can now work together toward a common goal of treating his depression. Also try to sync up with his mental health team, if he has one, and coordinate goals with them involved.

Having a goal and knowing that you are there to help will give him something to work toward. This will increase his chances of sticking to things like exercise programs and medication regimens. There may be days when he drops off of the routine or refuses to help you work with him toward his goals. But he will likely come around soon and continue to work with you.

If your loved one is resistant, you should never coerce him to do anything. He has free will. But you can influence him to lead a healthier lifestyle by buying only healthy food, trying to get him to the gym, and making other lifestyle changes for the whole family.

Chapter 4: Forming a Support Network

You are probably one of your loved one's sole supporters. Depressed people usually don't have very many friends because they become so socially withdrawn and keep to themselves. Also, they often break ties or stop talking to loved ones and then don't have the energy to rekindle an abandoned relationship. So if you are still in touch with your loved one with depression, you are certainly lucky and you are also probably incredibly important to him.

But one of the key treatments for depression is a positive social support network. These are people that the depression sufferer can turn to for positive reinforcement and help when he needs it. Sadly, most depression sufferers have very poor support networks. This is partly what can cause depression, but it is also what can occur as a result of depression. Therefore, it is a vicious cycle that your loved one may have trouble escaping. You can help him form that missing support network that extends beyond just you.

In addition, depression often drives sufferers to take up drug abuse and other unsafe habits. Shopping, gambling, unsafe sex with strangers, and other impulsive behaviors may become vices that your loved one engages in. With these vices come bad friends and negative influences who keep your loved one trapped in the cycle of depression and whatever vice he has fallen into.

One of the things that you can help your loved one with is helping him form a healthy, positive support network of people who actually care about him. You can help him discern who actually has his best interests at heart, and who he can turn to for help. You can also help him get out and meet people. Introduce him to good people that you know from the church, or any other form of community that you belong to.

It can be hard to get a depressed person to meet new friends. You don't have to force your loved one to go out. Instead, bring people to him. Have supportive, positive people come over to meet him. Bring people over and encourage him to talk to them to be polite. This will help bring him out of his shell.

The more that he is exposed to social contact, the more he will want more contact in the future. Now encourage him to go to church, take up a hobby, or volunteer somewhere. Remember from the previous chapter, always take baby steps. Some depressed individuals are able to maintain social contact and put on a normal face all through their struggle, while others are truly debilitated and cannot get out at all. Not all depressed people are severely introverted because of their illness, but some are. Only push your loved one as far as he can reasonably go when it comes to getting out and meeting people.

Sit down with him and ask him who in his life makes him feel better. Ask him who he feels comfortable turning to. Have him make a list of people that he can call if he feels lonely or suicidal. Make sure that he considers family and other people from his past that he has not spoken to in a while. Rekindling those bonds will help him feel so much better as he realizes that people do not actually hate him and he is in fact loved by many.

That's the next step. Have him make a list of people that he misses. Then encourage him to call them or text them. You can offer to stay by his side to make sure that the conversation goes well and he follows through with it.

Also, help him choose to get rid of people from his past and present who are unhealthy and negative. Help him recognize some of the toxic presences in his life. He will not always listen to you and dump certain bad influences, but you can certainly help him understand how his life could benefit from getting rid of certain people. Most likely he already knows who is bad for him but he is unwilling to end any of his current friendships for fear of being lonely. Therefore, you can nudge him in the right direction by pointing out better people that he can use to fill the void, so that he no longer needs his toxic friends.

You can't force your loved one with depression to do anything. But you can guide him in the right direction by introducing him to good people, encouraging him to start healthy activities, and offering your support no matter what.

Chapter 5: Try to Get Them Active

Your loved one will not want to be active if he is in the depths of depression. Depression robs people of energy and the desire to do anything that requires action, even if it is something that they formerly loved. Therefore, trying to motivate your loved one to get out and do something can sometimes seem like an impossible task. But it is not altogether impossible. Getting your depressed loved one active is essential for his recovery.

Really the best thing that you can do is to provide encouragement. You should also provide a healthy model. You cannot reasonably expect to influence your loved one to exercise or to get out if you just sit around on the couch all day yourself. If you are seen doing things, you might just push your loved one to do the same. He might become more active seeing you be active.

You should also find activities that your loved one would actually enjoy. Even if he doesn't feel up to it at first, over time he will start to feel the desire to get out and do something that he used to enjoy. He won't feel this way about an activity that he hates. What did he used to do? Was he into dancing, hiking, or volunteering with animals? Find what he used to love and gradually introduce that back into his life by getting involved yourself.

You can also use subtle techniques to urge him back into some activity. For instance, if he used to volunteer with animals, subscribe to some mailing lists from animal organizations like the ASPCA and the World Wildlife Fund. Leave this mail around where he can see it in order to plant the idea in his head. Also, offer lots of open encouragement. Say things like, "Didn't you used to volunteer at a shelter? Wouldn't it be nice if you did that again? You need to get out of the house and animals need help."

He may not respond at first, but at least the idea is now in his mind. It may make him want to get out and do something again. As he makes progress with medication and therapy and lifestyle changes, he may start to feel well enough to go out and do these things. The idea will grow and grow in his mind until he is well enough to do it.

Therapy will also help him get out there. Try to get him to see a therapist. Group therapy may even be better, as it will force him to talk to others and leave his comfort zone of reclusion. Support groups are great ways for him to build a positive social network of people who understand him and what he is going through. He will feel less alone if he goes to therapy and he will have a better shot at working through his issues.

You can also bring activities into his house. Games, either electronic or board games, can be a fun way to bond with your loved one and add some cheer to his life. Bring in something fun like Twister or Scrabble and encourage everyone in the family to gather for a rowdy game night. He might grumble or resist at first, but eventually he may join in, and have a great time with everyone. You can also bring him puzzles and do them with him. Have movie night, complete with popcorn and candy and all of the lights off. Do whatever you can to make activities in the home fun and stimulating.

Pets can be incredibly relieving and healing for people with depression. Bring in a pet if you don't already have one. Or take your loved one to the shelter to pick one out himself. A new pet can help him feel better and can distract him from his pain. It has been discovered that the act of petting animals like dogs and cats and horses can have a soothing effect on people. If he starts to take the pet for walks or to play, this will count as getting out as well. It will help him elevate his mood.

Your company is very important. Just being there accomplishes far more than it may appear. The two of you don't have to be extremely active or do anything fancy together for your company to make a difference in his mood. Just doing activities together like watching TV and discussing the episodes, doing puzzles, and other such activities do count. Your presence and the simple activity that you engage your loved one with both will occupy your loved one's mind, distract him from dwelling on his issues, and help him feel better. Having social contact and stimulating activities is essential for your loved one's healing. It will release serotonin and dopamine in his brain, which are feel-good hormones that correct depression when in the right balance.

Remember that your attempts may not work at first. Or they may work only a small percentage of the time. But keep trying and don't give up. Each time that you give your loved one something to do or to smile about, you give him at least a few minutes of relief from his depression. To someone who suffers from depression for most of the time, these few minutes can mean everything.

Chapter 6: Improve Diet and Exercise

This chapter really only applies if you live with someone who suffers from depression. If you share a residence with this person, then you can help subtly change and improve his lifestyle by offering healthier food options and by introducing exercise to everyone's routine. Even if your loved one insists on eating fast food and other junk food for emotional comfort, you have at least done your part by leaving healthier options around the house. At mealtimes, serve only healthy options so that your loved one is more likely to partake in some good food as he eats with the family. Even if you don't live with someone, you can subtly introduce better food to his diet by bringing by healthful snacks or meals that you prepared.

Exercise

Any kind of exercise is beneficial. Exercise and strenuous physical activity help the body burn off cortisol and adrenalin, stress hormones that increase depression if left unchecked. They can also release serotonin and help your loved one get proper sleep. Your loved one's self-esteem will improve as he notices his body changing and as he accomplishes feats of strength and endurance that he previously thought he could never accomplish.

But certain exercises are more beneficial than others. Usually, if your loved one is depressed, he has not worked out for some time.

Therefore, you should encourage him to start out with light exercise to build up his strength and prevent sports-related injuries. Beginner's yoga, beginner's Tai Chi, beginner's Pilates, and dance are forms of conditioning and strengthening exercises that are also proved to release stress and calm agitated nerves. Your loved one will feel so much better if he starts performing yoga or Tai Chi before bed, for instance. He will feel even better if you get him to join a group class, where he can be around other people and possibly socialize.

It is also best to encourage your loved one to perform exercise that makes the time pass by more rapidly. For instance, dance fitness can be so fun that he won't notice the passage of time. Soon enough, the exercise routine will conclude and he will be surprised that it is over already. He will decide that it's not so bad and he will be more likely to continue with the program. If you get him to try exercise that is repetitive, intense, and boring, the minutes will drag and he won't be as likely to continue doing it.

There may be an exercise that your loved one enjoys immensely. This is the one that you should encourage him to take up again. For instance, if he used to love lifting but he has quit because of the lack of motivation that depression brings, you can start a weight lifting program. Ask him, "Do you remember how much you used to love lifting at the gym? Well, I got a membership and I'd like you to come along and show me the ropes." This is a subtle way to trick him into going back to the exercise that he used to love.

Foods that Fight Depression

Believe it or not, there are some foods that specifically target and fight depression and other psychiatric disorders. These foods are great at balancing hormones and chemicals in the body while also correcting deficiencies that commonly lead to depression. Eating more of these foods are likely to help your loved one feel much better.

Asparagus is a rich source of folic acid. Folic acid is often lacking in depression patients, so try fixing asparagus at least once a week. Steam it to preserve its nutritional content.

Avocado is rich with B vitamins. B vitamins are linked to nervous health. Most people with psychiatric problems are also deficient in different B vitamins. Also, avocado contains natural fatty acids, which help in the production of DNA and RNA in your cells. They are also filling, so they discourage your loved one from stuffing his face with junk food later on.

Mushrooms contain vitamin D. Vitamin D increases energy and vitality in your loved one, so make mushrooms with butter, stuffed mushrooms, or mushroom patties for dinner sometimes. As a side note, having your loved one get out into the sun will also up his vitamin D naturally. Sadly, most people don't get enough sunlight to fulfill their vitamin D needs.

Blueberries contain tons of antioxidants and vitamin C. They can help your loved one naturally process stress hormones and feel better. They also taste great, so your loved one can enjoy them in place of junk food. Make smoothies or sprinkle blueberries on cereal or yogurt for breakfast.

Milk has calcium and potassium. This can help with your loved one's energy levels and the muscle spasms and aches that often accompany depression. Dairy products will also give him more energy. He can enjoy cheese snacks instead of junk food and fruity or chocolaty Greek yogurt instead of sweets. Yogurt parfaits are also a filling treat that offer him fiber and the benefits of fruit as well.

Salmon has Omega 3 fatty acids which dramatically help improve mood health. It also has iron and zinc in appropriately low levels. Sometimes it can even have mercury, which in extremely low levels is actually good for the body. These nutrients provide natural energy and stress regulation. Your loved one will feel a lot better after eating salmon filets or sushi rolls with raw salmon inside. He can eat canned salmon for a snack. Plus, salmon will feel like a special treat to him because it is so yummy.

Spinach has enough magnesium to account for forty percent of your diet. Magnesium is essential for depression relief. It is known to regulate your stress hormones and make you feel well. Cooking can kill the magnesium, so try steaming spinach instead.

Almonds have B vitamins and Vitamin E. They provide lots of natural energy and depression relief. Have your loved one eat them by the handful or add shaved almonds to meals. Use almond milk rather than soy milk.

Oranges are hearty sources of Vitamin C. They help your loved one feel calmer as the vitamin C helps him handle stress better. Orange juice often contains sufficient vitamin C for someone's daily allotment.

Bananas are rich in potassium, which can relieve muscle aches and increase muscle health. They also provide fast energy because of their high sugar content. This is a healthy sugar, however, which does not cause a crash later one like candy or other processed sugars.

Dark chocolate has antioxidants which help you handle stress and anxiety, two factors that often contribute to depression. Bring lots of dark chocolate for your loved one. Better yet, bring him dark chocolate bars with almonds, peanuts, or orange in them for added benefits.

Alcohol is a depressant and therefore is not very advisable for depressed people. However, a good red wine has antioxidants that can be incredibly helpful in improving mood health. A glass a day or a few glasses a week can really help your loved one. A glass of wine can also relax him and help him sleep, aiding in the relief of sleep problems that pervade people with depression.

Eggs have B vitamins which can improve your depression. They also have lots of good cholesterol and protein, which improve mood health and energy by increasing muscle health and blood circulation. Plus, eggs are easy to make and you can find a variety of recipes for eggs.

Legumes are rich in B vitamins and folic acid. Eat a lot of beans, peas, and peanuts. Add this stuff to your cooking. Always accompany meals with a side of beans or peas. Keep a jar of peanuts around for snacking. Peanut butter can work too.

Beef, pork, and chicken all contain B and A vitamins to help boost your mood. They are also protein-rich, and thus they are sources of growth and sustained energy throughout the day. Try to avoid frying meat, as this removes nutrition, and instead grill, boil, or broil your meats.

Micronutrients

Micronutrients are one of those mysterious things that seem to hold the answer to curing depression, though scientists don't quite understand why yet. Certain vitamins and minerals are very helpful for depression. Sometimes they even totally cure someone's depression issues.

One of the main vitamins that will give your loved one energy and vitality is vitamin B. There are many forms of vitamin B, but niacin or a Vitamin B Complex will be the most effective in treating his depression. He can also get vitamin B from consuming meat, along with vitamin A and iron. Folic acid has also been associated with depression; a folic acid tablet, prenatal vitamins with folic acid, or eating foods rich in folic acid will improve his mood and concentration exponentially. Calcium and magnesium are two crucial minerals that he can get from consuming dairy or taking additional supplements. Antioxidants found in blueberries, wine, and even fish are also important. Even just a good multivitamin should help him develop more energy and a better mood.

A lot of micronutrients come from one's diet. But unfortunately, many foods no longer contain as much nutrition as they once did because of depleted soil, pesticides, growth hormones, genetic engineering, and other unnatural food production methods. Therefore, many people are lacking in the micronutrients that they need. Also, many people do not eat very healthfully, and instead eat junk food, which has zero nutritional content. Seek help from supplements to make up for what your loved one's diet lacks.

Make sure that you buy a good supplements or supplements and make sure that your loved one takes them every day along with his antidepressant medication. You would also benefit from taking these supplements and preventing yourself from developing depression due to a vitamin or mineral deficiency.

Provide Plenty of Water

Always have water handy. If your loved one is resistant to drinking water, then just offer him water at every chance that you get. Serve a glass of water with meals. This is how you can get him to drink water without him realizing what you are doing. Don't offer him soda and certainly don't offer him alcohol, unless it is a high-quality red wine, which contains antioxidants that are very important to his mood health. Dehydration can lead to poor mood, irritability, and lack of energy, so supplying your loved one with plenty of water can actually improve his mood health. Even if more water is not the cure, it will certainly make things easier and better for your loved one.

Encourage Good Hygiene

How can you get your loved one to bathe and maintain his house? Gentle encouragement is usually the best way. You can't force him to stay clean, but if you urge him to take a bath, he might. Many people who become severely depressed cannot manage their health or their hygiene. If you are there as a voice of reason, you may be able to get him to take care of himself better.

Chapter 7: Become a Model of Positivity

You cannot directly change someone else's behavior. If you do, you will likely be met with defensiveness and resistance. It is far better to subtly influence the person's behavior to become better for you. As you likely know by now, this is incredibly hard to do with someone who is suffering from depression. Your efforts may have been totally unsuccessful. But the best that you can do for yourself and your loved one is to live your life in a healthy and positive way. This way, you create a sort of model for the depressed individual.

You should also take care of yourself and live the life that you want, regardless of whether or not it affects your depressed loved one at all. This is an essential part of self-care. You can't neglect yourself and expect to maintain the level of sanity needed to help someone else. Sometimes, you need to tend to your needs first. I cover this more in Chapter 9.

Being a model does not mean that you need to be perfect. Rather, it means that you show your loved one that is OK to not be perfect, but that he still needs to try to live well. You show him that it is OK to mess up and that he should not beat himself up over failures or mistakes, as these things are only human. You show him how it is to behave normally again.

You also inspire him to live better. By living a good life yourself, you show him how a good life looks. This may inspire him to want to live this life himself. He will want to join you on fun excursions, outings with friends, volunteer causes, and even a healthier lifestyle.

If you live with a person with depression, then his depression may rub off on you. Don't let it get you down. Keep living the life that you want. By being active and living life to the fullest, you add positive energy to your loved one's life. This helps him feel better and more positive himself.

You can also influence his lifestyle by having healthy food and snacks around. You can prevent him from staying in bed all day and you can encourage him to exercise with you. Finally, you can bring healthy friends over, which will help him learn not to keep the toxic and harmful company that he may keep.

Again, you don't have to be perfect. Your life is not all about your loved one with depression. You can make mistakes and have bad habits of your own. But the healthier your life is, the better you will feel. And the better you can make your loved one feel, too. You can work on your own self-improvement while working on uplifting your loved one.

Chapter 8: Always Be Supportive

The most important thing to keep in mind with a depressed loved one is that consistency is essential for his healing. This means that you need to always be supportive. You don't want to be the billionth person to abandon him, as this abandonment could seriously push him over the edge into despair or even suicide. You need to consistently be there for him and never cease to support him in his healing.

Sometimes, it can be hard. You may want to walk away and give up. However, it is better to just take a break when you feel this way. Don't give up on your loved one. Just take a walk, a brief vacation, or even a spa day where you

pamper yourself. Care for yourself and rest. But
don't run away.

Offer Support

Every step of the way, be there for your
loved one. Let him know that he can rely on you
for support. Tell him that you love him and that
you are always there. Abstain from offering
judgment or criticism or even advice. Just be a
quiet support pillar for your loved one.

Dealing with Medication Issues

Sometimes, certain medications don't
work. They may cause your loved one to suffer
from serious side effects, they may make him
suicidal, they may make him feel better at first
then suddenly stop working, or they may have no
effect at all. Your loved one will probably go

through a period of experimentation, where he tries various medications in the search for the right one. This period can be stressful for both your loved one and you. You have to watch out for bad symptoms, you have to make sure that your loved one doesn't hurt himself, and you have to make many trips to the psychiatrist's office.

Be there for your loved one. Let him know that he can tell you if he is feeling weird. Make sure that he knows that you won't judge him harshly. Also make sure that he knows that it can be very dangerous for him to ignore his feelings, so he should let you know and call his psychiatrist if he ever starts to feel off while taking a new medication.

Also try to avoid venting your frustrations to your loved one or you may make him feel guilty for bothering you with his problems. If you do get frustrated, take it out with intense exercise or take it out on a punching bag. Find someone that you can talk to, either another loved one or a therapist, so that you can unburden yourself from the bad emotions that undoubtedly arise from your trials and tribulations with your depressed loved one. Never tell your loved one about these negative emotions, however. You don't want to burden him with any more pain than he already goes through with his condition.

Symptoms

The symptoms of depression can literally ruin your relationship if you let them. However, you can deal with these symptoms better if you always keep in mind that none of your loved one's behavior is personally directed at you. Your loved one may act like a jerk or may neglect your relationship, but this is not intentional. If you stick by his side and show him that you are always there, you can really reduce his depression. You can also enjoy his improved behavior once he feels better.

When your loved one's behavior gets to be too much, it's time to step away. Go out with other people who provide you with the comfort and social stimulation that your loved one cannot. Also, rely on others to help you cope with the frustration and even pain that may arise after you spend some time around your love one fighting his depression along with him. Have people to talk to who can walk you through your emotions and help you release your anguish. Expressing yourself to others will make you feel better, so that you can return to your loved one with a smile on your face and a refreshed mind.

It is also important to realize that not all of your loved one's symptoms are things that you can treat or manage. Some things are solely his responsibility. He will only get well and manage his symptoms if he chooses to. You can influence him and support him, but you can't heal him yourself. That is a task that he must undertake himself. Don't get frustrated if he refuses to seek help or to address certain issues that he suffers from. If he exhibits certain symptoms that you cannot deal with, don't fight and try to help him in ways that you cannot. This will only backfire.

Instead, let him work through some things himself. Talk to him about what he's feeling, encourage him to talk to you, and nudge him in the right direction. That is literally all that you can do. Don't take too much upon yourself, or you will exhaust yourself and burn out. You will also feel like a failure as you can't help your loved one in certain ways.

Backslides

One of the most discouraging things about dealing with a loved one with depression is backslides. Your loved one may start to get well. He may start to feel better and act better. You think that everything is finally going to be OK. Then, suddenly, he can't get out of bed. Or something bad happens and he falls off the wagon again. Or he relapses on drugs. Whatever happens, it may seem that his progress is wasted and he is back to square one. And you may feel that all of your efforts have been in vain and that this nightmare will never end for either of you.

Unfortunately, backslides are an almost inevitable part of depression. Depression rarely ever totally lifts. People can treat it and manage it quite effectively, but a majority of people never actually cure it. Returning to depression after a period of wellness is something that is quite likely to happen. Relapses into drug use are also a very common and likely part of the road to sobriety, especially if your loved one's emotional issues that lie at the core of his depression have not been addressed.

But you can lessen the likelihood and severity of depression backslides by getting your loved one help. Medication will help buoy his mood and mental stability. Therapy will teach him to cope with his symptoms so that they are not as horrible. A book or other guide for managing depression can also help teach him coping skills so that he does not fall into a deep pit of depression whenever his depression kicks in again. A good diet, exercise, and vitamin supplements can certainly improve his health and decrease his likelihood of recurring episodes.

Also, your loved one needs to work on himself and he needs to try to address the deep-seated issues or scars that may lie at the bottom of his depression. Sometimes depression is caused by purely physical problems, such as thyroid issues or diabetes. In these cases, depression is more of a side effect or symptom than a condition on its own. These physical conditions can be managed to effectively treat the depression. However, if someone's depression is not caused by physical issues and seems to be recurring or chronic, there is probably a negative self-belief or thinking pattern that keeps his depression around. He is more negative than he should be, which causes him to think harmful thoughts and develop the chemical imbalance that leads to depression symptoms. He also probably has repressed pain or memories that manifest as depression. His depression will never be cured until he addresses these issues and gets over them. Often, he can only do this with the guidance of a good therapist, or with intense amounts of self-work and journal writing and meditation. He will only work on himself if he wants to. You can always encourage him to undertake this task, but you can't ever force him.

Chapter 9: Self-care Tips

For the past several chapters, we have talked about how to help your loved one through the misery of depression. But sometimes it may feel that everything is about your loved one. Now let's take some time to focus on you. It is about you, too, and you need care just as much as your depressed loved one does. So let's talk about ways that you can cope and take care of yourself while living with a person who is afflicted by depression.

Know Your Limits

No one can bear everything on their own. You already bear a rather heavy cross. If your loved one pushes you too far with his behavior or his demands, understand that it is normal to reach a point where you cannot extend any further. Understand that you have limits to what you can do and what you can handle. Don't be afraid to say no when necessary.

Learning when to say no is essential to your own health. If you don't feel comfortable with something, say so. If you feel hurt, speak up. Refuse to take on tasks that you know that you can't handle.

There may be many reasons why something crosses your limits. Perhaps you have a full-time job and can't handle also spending massive amounts of time with your loved one. That's fine. Just spend as much time as you can. You don't have to be there for him 24/7. Or perhaps you are emotionally sensitive and some of his actions really hurt your feelings. You can refuse to do things with him that you know will cause him to act out and hurt you.

Your limits are not unreasonable. You are not a bad person for not wanting or being able to do everything that your loved one asks of you. It is OK to put your foot down and say no sometimes. It is also OK to take a break or walk away for a little while when your emotions build up to a boiling point.

Set Boundaries

Just because your loved one is sick mentally does not mean that he can walk all over you. You need to establish certain boundaries to protect your own interests and sanity. You can set limits on what he can ask of you, how much time you spend with him, and what you are willing to do for him. You are not his slave, so you can say no whenever you need.

You also can set clear rules for how he can speak to you. If he snaps at you or otherwise mistreats you, understand that this is probably because of his illness. But nevertheless, you don't have to take this treatment. Tell him to be nice to you. Inform him that he cannot get away with speaking to you that way. You can even walk away for a while and take a break, to show him that you mean business. Never let him cross your boundaries. He needs to respect you and be nice.

Your personal time and space is important. You need to tend to yourself, too. If he tries to invade your space and time because he is overly reliant on you, gently remind him that you need your space and time clear for a little while. Let him know that you love him and you will help him when it is time for you two to hang out again. You can limit the times when he can call you and you can limit when you will see him or do things for him, such as shopping or chores.

Take Time for Yourself

This is your life. You don't need to put it on hold for your loved one. Continue to live your life and do the things that you love. Go out on dates or go do your favorite hobbies. Meet up with friends and be social. Spend time alone at home, decompressing. Read books and watch movies. Not everything needs to revolve around your loved one. You need to have your own life separate from your loved one, or you will quickly burn out on care giving and his company.

Depressed individuals are not always fun to be around. Taking a break is essential for you to get past the negativity that your loved one may emit. Spend time recharging by yourself or with positive people. Use this time to decompress and clear your head. This will prevent you from getting frustrated with your loved one and tired of his attitude and depression symptoms.

Every once in a while, you need to treat yourself to a day of pampering. Really treat yourself. Go to the spa or the salon or barbershop. Take a little trip. Buy yourself something nice. You deserve it after the emotional burden that you deal with every day. Treating yourself is an act of self-love that can help you avoid falling into depression yourself.

Make your health a priority. Taking care of yourself will also prevent you from developing depression yourself.

Seek Help when You Need It

No one can bear every burden completely on their own. You can seek help if you need it.

Find other people who can help you care for your loved one. Have other people who will visit him, try to get him out, and assist him with chores or emotional support. Have other people who will check on him and see if he is going to work and school and feeling all right. Use a support system of people to help take care of him.

Also, seek help for yourself. Even if you do not suffer from any mental illness, living with someone who is mentally ill can expose to you a lot of toxic speech and thinking. You may develop a lot of harmful emotions and thoughts yourself after spending lots of time with this individual. Find someone that you can talk to so that you can let these feelings out and process them in a healthy way without developing depression yourself. Therapists are always confidential and you don't have to worry about your complaining getting back to your depressed loved one and making him feel worse. Or find a good friend who will listen to you and be discreet as well.

Conclusion

Depression is horrible for everyone involved. You may suffer just as much as your loved one with depression does. Don't ever let anyone dismiss the level of your pain and strength as you fight this battle alongside your loved one. This is your war too.

You are an admirable person to take on the task of caring for your loved one with depression. Most people would not be able to handle this and would give up. You are exhibiting incredible strength and resilience and compassion. You are also providing your loved one the best service possible, by not abandoning him.

Of course, no one said this job would be easy. You have done the right thing by reading this book. This book can help you navigate the difficult task of caring for your depressed loved one and coping with the bad emotions that commonly arise in connection with dealing with another person's depression. This book can help you ward off depression yourself by taking care of yourself and learning your limits.

This job may never be entirely easy. You will struggle as much as your loved one does with his illness. However, this book's advice will help ease some of the challenges that you may face. It will certainly make living with someone with depression a little bit better because you will be able to understand and handle this person's problems more effectively.

Never forget to be patient. If you start to lose your patience, take some time off. Don't give up or take your anger out on your depressed loved one. You have to be very conscious and careful about your speech and actions regarding this loved one. He is in a tender place in life, and you must make sure not to worsen his condition. However, this does not mean that you should ever neglect yourself. Your needs are important too. Don't put your life on hold for this person. Continue to live your life and give yourself fulfillment beyond just helping your loved one cope.

Relapses and backslides will happen. There will be other unforeseen challenges, as well. You may get overwhelmed. Learn when to step away or seek help. But continue to offer your support and try to keep a smile on your face. Be a model of positivity for your loved one, who is in a very negative place.

Congratulations to you for being a caregiver, and thank you for your help. Your loved one needs you and appreciates you more than you will ever know. Just keep that in mind when the going gets tough. And never be afraid to refer to this book for help and advice.

CPSIA information can be obtained
at www.ICGtesting.com
Printed in the USA
BVOW03s2143261017
498791BV00001B/2/P